Pioneers

MALCOLM X

rourke biographies

Pioneers

MALCOLM X

by
KIBIBI MACK-WILLIAMS

Rourke Publications, Inc.
Vero Beach, Florida 32964

Library of Congress Cataloging-in-Publication Data
Mack-Williams, Kibibi, 1955-
    Malcolm X / written by Kibibi Mack-Williams.
        p.   cm. — (Rourke biographies. Pioneers)
    Includes bibliographical references and index.
    Summary: Presents the life, philosophy, assassination,
and legacy of the African American leader who advocated
black nationalism.
    ISBN 0-86625-493-5 (alk. paper)
    1. X, Malcolm, 1925-1965—Juvenile literature.   2.
Black Muslims—Biography—Juvenile literature. 3. Afro-
Americans—Biography—Juvenile literature.   [1. X, Malcolm, 1925-1965.   2. Afro-Americans—Biography.]   I.
Title. II. Series.
BP223.Z8L5762   1993
320.5′4′092—dc20
    [B]   92-46767
                                                   CIP
                                                   AC

473156

Contents

Color Illustrations

Pioneers

MALCOLM X

Chapter 1

El-Hajj Malik El-Shabazz

He was born Malcolm Little. He became known to millions of people as Malcolm X. The name on his coffin was El-Hajj Malik El-Shabazz, an Islamic name which he took after making a pilgrimage to Mecca in 1964. Who was Malcolm X? He was a man who, in his short life, never stopped changing, never stopped questioning, never made peace with the way things are for African Americans.

A History of Injustice

African Americans have fought against prejudice since they first came to the United States as slaves in the 1600's. Even free African Americans living during the period of slavery still felt enslaved because their skin color did not allow them to escape prejudice and discrimination. Both slaves and free African Americans were prohibited from living equally with whites. Regarded as members of an inferior race, they were deprived of education, forced to live in separate, segregated areas, and given only the worst jobs. They did not have political rights or legal protection in the court system.

Despite the often brutal forces ranged against them, the slaves did not passively accept their condition. By various means, ranging from rebellion and escape to more subtle forms of resistance, the slaves rejected their unequal status. At the same time, sympathetic whites worked together with free African Americans to end slavery and gain civil rights for all African Americans.

In the decades after slavery was abolished in 1865, African Americans still were not equal to whites. American society

11

continued to be rigidly segregated, keeping the races separate
and unequal. Most African Americans continued to have the
lowest-paying jobs, lived in the worst housing, were the least
educated, and were prevented from voting, even though they
had a legal right to vote. Many lived in fear of losing their
lives if accused of any minor wrongdoing. In the South
especially, up to the 1960's, whites who beat or even murdered
African Americans were rarely convicted of any crime.

The average African-American family taught their children
to "stay in their places" and never offend any whites,
regardless of their age. Even though many whites did not
respect African Americans and felt they were superior to them,
African Americans had to show the utmost respect to all
whites. African-American parents wanted a different life for
their children. They hoped and prayed for a society that would

Civil rights demonstrators in Birmingham, Alabama in 1963. (AP/Wide World Photos)

be free of racial discrimination and filled with equal opportunities for all races. In the meantime, many African Americans continued to work in different ways to bring about such a society.

In the segregated South, it was customary for African Americans to ride in the back of the bus or, if the bus was crowded, to give their seats to white passengers. In 1955, Rosa Parks, an African-American woman living in Montgomery, Alabama, refused to give up her seat to a white passenger. As a result, she was arrested. This incident caused the African Americans in the city to unite under the leadership of Dr. Martin Luther King, Jr., and refuse to ride the city buses until the system was fully desegregated. The Montgomery Bus Boycott marked the beginning of the Civil Rights movement in the United States. It was during this time that Malcolm X emerged as one of the new leaders seeking solutions to help improve social conditions for African Americans.

Black Nationalism

Malcolm X first attained national prominence as a spokesperson for the Nation of Islam. Sometimes referred to as "Black Muslims," members of the Nation of Islam did not participate in the Civil Rights movement. They were black nationalists and did not believe in integration. Instead, they wanted to build a separate African-American nation within the United States. It was within this organization that Malcolm X emerged as one of the greatest African-American leaders in the twentieth century.

The Nation of Islam had a major impact as an alternative to the Civil Rights movement. Young activists, in particular, were attracted to its black nationalism. Malcolm X, the Nation of Islam's most influential speaker, encouraged African Americans to love themselves and be proud of their African heritage. He was responsible for radicalizing young

13

African-American activists as he continued to advocate black nationalism and self-defense.

Many African-American youths criticized the moderate Civil Rights leaders and their philosophy of nonviolence. As the passive resistance of Civil Rights workers was increasingly met by verbal insults, police dogs, water hoses, riot sticks, beatings, and murders, these black youths wanted to fight back. They also rejected the goal of integration and discouraged white participation in their organizations and programs. Like Malcolm, they became black nationalists and asserted self-determination and pride in their heritage and culture.

Malcolm's travels to the Middle East, Africa, and Europe further developed his ideas. He learned more about orthodox Islam, and the ways in which its teachings differed from those of the Black Muslims. During this time Malcolm also helped to make people in other countries more aware of the cruel sufferings that African Americans continued to experience in the United States. He even tried to bring these problems before the United Nations.

Malcolm was different from many prominent leaders during the Civil Rights era because he spoke up without fear. He said many things that other African Americans would not publicly say for fear of losing their jobs or even their lives. He committed his entire adult life to bringing about change for his people. Malcolm's own ideas continued to evolve right up to the time of his assassination in 1965.

The Many Sides of Malcolm X

Malcolm's impact did not end with his death. In fact, Malcolm is probably more widely known and more influential in the 1990's than at any time since the 1960's. Spike Lee's popular movie, *Do the Right Thing*, helped to spark a surge of interest in Malcolm. Lee's movie, which contains several

Malcolm X was fearless in his attacks on racism; he spoke out at a time when many were silent. (Library of Congress)

references to Malcolm, concludes with a controversial quote from Malcolm's speech, "The Ballot or the Bullet." Even more influential was Lee's 1992 film, *Malcolm X*, which brought Malcolm's life story to millions of people, though some critics have charged that Lee's portrait of Malcolm is superficial and in some respects seriously distorted. Malcolm's picture, a quote from one of his speeches, or simply the symbol "X" could be seen on hats, bags, shirts, and other items. Malcolm was everywhere.

The renewed interest in Malcolm's life and thought has not been limited to young people who are discovering him for the first time. There also has been an increase in scholarly publications on Malcolm—articles, books, and dissertations. Musical artists include lines or film clips from Malcolm's speeches in their lyrics and videos. Various organizations have held public memorials on his birthday, while others have produced documentary films on his life.

This resurgence has opened new discussion of Malcolm's ideas and their relevance today. How would Malcolm approach the concerns of the African-American community in the 1990's? There are many different answers to that question. One group may focus on the Malcolm who advocated violence, if necessary, in the struggle for African-American liberation. Another group may focus on Malcolm the black separatist. For yet another group, Malcolm's commitment to Islam is central. Each group claims that their Malcolm is the real Malcolm. Perhaps each of these interpretations of Malcolm's life and work carries part—but only a part—of the truth.

Malcolm's own account of his life can be found in *The Autobiography of Malcolm X*, written by Alex Haley (see appendix, "Speeches and Writings of Malcolm X"). Read by millions, Malcolm's autobiography has been acclaimed as a classic of twentieth-century literature. Recent studies, while not ignoring Malcolm's autobiography, have sought to document his life in a more systematic way, sometimes contradicting Malcolm's account.

While there is debate among scholars concerning some of the facts of Malcolm's life as presented in *The Autobiography of Malcolm X*, this book will frequently rely on the autobiography as a source of information—in particular, as the primary source for information about Malcolm's childhood—and his recollections will generally be regarded as accurate.

Chapter 2

Lansing

Malcolm's parents were Earl and Louise Little. His father, Earl Little, was born in Reynolds, Georgia. As a boy, Earl worked on his father's farm and had very little formal education. At that time, it was common for African Americans in the South to move to the North to seek better economic opportunities and to escape the harsh work of sharecropping and the terror of the Ku Klux Klan (KKK). Around 1900, when Earl reached young manhood, he joined the parade of African Americans migrating from the South. He first became a Baptist minister in Philadelphia, Pennsylvania, and, later, a dedicated organizer for Marcus Garvey's black nationalist organization, the Universal Negro Improvement Association (UNIA).

Malcolm's mother was born Louise Norton in Grenada, West Indies. She was an interracial child, born to a white father and black mother. A beautiful woman, she had long black hair that hung to her waist and was so light-skinned that she was often mistaken for being white. Unlike her husband, Earl, Louise had attended school as a young girl and could read and write well. Like her husband, she, too, had been a part of a migratory wave of people in search of opportunity in the North.

Before he met Louise, Earl Little had been married once and had three children by that previous marriage. However, he had separated from his wife when he moved to Montreal, Canada. It was there that he met Louise and fell in love with her. Shortly after their meeting, Louise became Earl's second wife.

The Garvey Movement

Both Earl and Louise were black nationalists who were very proud of their African heritage. They followed the teachings of Marcus Garvey, the most influential pan-Africanist of the early twentieth century. Garvey taught that all black people of African descent shared an identity as Africans first and foremost. He encouraged African Americans to take pride in their race, culture, and history. He believed that they should start their own businesses, schools, and churches and should one day return to their true homeland, Africa.

Earl and Louise moved to Philadelphia, where they had their first child. They later moved to Omaha, Nebraska, where their next three children were born, including Malcolm. Malcolm Little was born May 19, 1925. Unlike the other children, he was born with blue-green eyes and light red hair, and he inherited his mother's light-skinned complexion.

Malcolm's parents continued to be active in the Garvey movement. His father was president of the Omaha chapter of the UNIA. Earl Little traveled around Omaha and to other surrounding towns to recruit more African-American members into the organization. His activities infuriated whites in the area to the point where hooded Klansmen rode by one night, yelling warnings for the troublemaker, Earl Little, to get out of town. To protect his family and avoid death, Earl Little moved the family after Malcolm's birth. They first relocated to Wisconsin and later, in 1929, to Lansing, Michigan. Earl Little remembered clearly the experiences of some of his uncles who had been killed by whites.

At first, the Littles moved into an old, two-story farmhouse on the outskirts of Lansing. Malcolm's father continued preaching and spreading the ideas of Marcus Garvey. Soon afterward, the Black Legionnaires, a white organization that wore black robes, threatened the family. When the Littles' house was firebombed, Earl knew it was time to leave. From

19

there, they moved to East Lansing, where Earl Little built a four-room house for his family. This was where Malcolm spent his boyhood days growing up.

Earl Little would take his young son, Malcolm, with him in his old black car when he traveled to preach in storefront churches in Michigan, Wisconsin, and Illinois. As a child, Malcolm also accompanied his father to Garveyite meetings and listened to the speeches his father made about Africa and the people of African descent living in the United States. At home, his father encouraged Malcolm and the other children to aspire to high goals in life.

Tragedy

Malcolm was six years old when his father died in 1931. When Earl Little did not return home after nightfall, Malcolm's mother was worried that something terrible might have happened to him. In the middle of the night, Malcolm awoke to his mother's screaming. She had received news from the police that her husband had been hit and run over by a streetcar. The circumstances surrounding his death suggested to many that Earl was murdered by the Black Legionnaires and then thrown across the railroad tracks. Now, Malcolm's mother was an unemployed widow with seven young children to support. The Great Depression was beginning, during which millions of people in the United States would lose their jobs and suffer from extreme poverty.

When Louise Little attempted to collect the money due her from her husband's life-insurance policy, the company refused to give her the money at first because they argued that his death was a suicide. She finally collected the money, and after it was slowly spent, she began to work as a maid. On occasion, she was able to get better paying jobs in stores because the owners thought she was white. Once they realized that she was not, they would fire her.

Police outside the Audubon Ballroom apprehend Talmadge Hayer, one of three Nation of Islam members convicted of murder for the assassination of Malcolm X. He died violently at the hands of others, staying committed to his beliefs—just like his father. (AP/Wide World Photos)

The Little family had become extremely poor. The children's clothes were clean but tattered. There was little or no food to eat in the house; many times, Malcolm and his brothers would walk several miles to get free bread from the welfare relief stores that helped people during the Depression. Malcolm's mother was a very proud woman and would refuse charity from her neighbors or the state welfare authorities. At school, a few of the more fortunate children would share their lunch with Malcolm. But because of his family's pride, many times he would not accept it.

By 1934, Malcolm's family was suffering terribly from the Depression. They often went hungry. His mother began to accept the welfare relief checks. Also, the older boys found small jobs and gave their earnings to their mother to help the family.

Despite these hardships, Malcolm enjoyed typical boyhood pursuits, playing baseball, hockey, football, and soccer with his friends. In school, he was a very bright student and loved to read. However, as he grew older he began to get in trouble more frequently—perhaps in part as a result of stresses and deprivation at home: the loss of his father, chronic hunger, and the increasing inability of his mother to cope with the demands of everyday life. In contrast to his early years, he began to perform poorly in school; as a result, he had to repeat the sixth grade. He was caught stealing several times, and the welfare authorities began to pressure Louise Little to put the children into foster homes.

Unable to care for her children as she once did and unable to come to terms with her husband's death, Mrs. Little began to withdraw and stay to herself. She continued to encourage the children to do well in school, but she began neglecting them. Mrs. Little refused to receive charitable help again, and the children were both hungry and poorly clothed. In 1939, Mrs. Little was committed to a state mental hospital in

Kalamazoo, Michigan, where she would remain for twenty-five years (in 1964, she was released in the care of her son, Philbert). At first, Malcolm's older siblings took care of the family, but later they became wards of the state.

By the time he was in the eighth grade, Malcolm had been placed in the Ingham County juvenile home in Mason, Michigan, not far from Lansing. It must have been difficult for Malcolm to be separated from his brothers and sisters, but in some ways the new setting was good for him. For the first time in his life, he had a room of his own. More important, though, was the affection and encouragement of Lois Swerlein, the cheerful, energetic housemother of the juvenile home.

Malcolm liked Mrs. Swerlein very much, responding well to her support, and worked very hard at his chores. He attended an all-white junior high school in Mason, where he applied himself to his schoolwork. His grades improved, and he became popular at school.

While living in the juvenile home, Malcolm met his half-sister, Ella, for the first time. Ella was one of Earl Little's children from his first marriage. She lived in Boston and wanted to see how her half-brothers and sisters were doing. Malcolm liked Ella right away. He admired her independence and strong will. In turn, she was very proud of Malcolm's achievements at school and felt he would achieve great success one day.

Ella invited Malcolm to visit her in Boston for the summer. When Malcolm arrived in Boston in 1939, he was overwhelmed with the Roxbury area where she lived. He admired the achievements of African Americans who owned their own homes and businesses. He was particularly impressed with the economic success of his sister, who also owned her own house and business and resided in a well-to-do African-American neighborhood.

Negative Encouragement

Malcolm's classmates respected him and saw him as a natural leader. They elected him to serve as their eighth-grade class president. One day, Malcolm was alone in the classroom with one of his teachers. His teacher asked him about the type of career he wanted to have once he finished school. Malcolm told him that he wanted to be a lawyer. Quickly, his teacher discouraged him and suggested that he might consider being a carpenter. He told Malcolm this was a more realistic aspiration for an African American. Carpentry was an acceptable job for African Americans because they could perform it without challenging white sterotypes.

After being encouraged to excel all his life, this advice was devastating to young Malcolm. He did not question his teacher's judgment; instead, he abandoned his goal of becoming a lawyer. He was deeply hurt, especially when he observed that his teacher did not advise the white students to abandon their career dreams. After this conversation, Malcolm's attitude toward school gradually changed. In his autobiography, Malcolm himself admitted that after this incident, he "just gave up."

Malcolm focused less on doing his schoolwork and concentrated more on playing sports. His attitude toward his school friends and teachers changed as well. He now preferred spending time on street corners with new friends who had no interest in schooling. In school, he started getting into trouble. He withdrew further from his classmates and stayed to himself more. Mrs. Swerlein, who had always admired Malcolm's liveliness and ambition, was unable to understand his changed behavior.

Malcolm decided that after he completed eighth grade, he would be finished with school. He felt that schooling was unnecessary since African Americans would only be hired for certain jobs that required little skill. When school ended for the summer, Malcolm wrote Ella asking if he could come live with her in Boston. Ella happily said yes. When Malcolm left for Boston, Ella had no way of knowing that his teacher's thoughtless racism had drastically changed his attitude toward school and life.

Chapter 3

Sister Ella

Malcolm arrived in Boston at age fifteen. Ella had high hopes for him. She knew of his ambitions to become a lawyer one day and wanted to prepare him for middle-class living. She made certain he associated with the nicer children in her neighborhood. Ella herself had very little education and was quite pleased to have a role in shaping Malcolm. She constantly gave him little talks to raise his confidence. When she learned of Malcolm's plans not to continue his schooling, she was extremely disappointed. Yet, she never gave up hope that he would one day change and make something good of his life.

The Street Life

Malcolm was anxious to meet new friends but found he did not easily fit in with upper-middle-class boys and girls. In fact, he was sometimes teased because of his clothing or his unsophisticated behavior. In the meantime, he started exploring other parts of the Roxbury area and eventually befriended some of the poorer boys in the neighborhood. These encounters gradually introduced him to another side of Roxbury, the glitter of the street life.

Malcolm's streetwise education really began at a Roxbury pool hall, where he made friends with one of the workers, a man named Shorty. Malcolm's new friend taught him how to gamble, how to buy clothes on credit, and even how to pick up black or white prostitutes. Before long, Malcolm had fully entered the hoodlum life, smoking marijuana (usually called "reefer"), gambling, and wearing his fashionable new clothes, especially the flamboyant "zoot suit." He adopted hipster slang and, to complete his new image, had his hair "conked" (straightened). Because the chemicals used in this process made his hair appear redder, he was later called "Detroit Red."

Ella did not approve of Malcolm's new friends nor his new image. She coaxed him to strive for a more respectable life. She was even more disappointed when he accepted a job as a shoeshine boy at the Roseland State Ballroom. In spite of the low pay, Malcolm was excited to have the job. This was during the era of swing music, and all the big band stars performed there. Malcolm took pleasure in meeting and shining the shoes of such great entertainers as Count Basie, Glenn Miller, Cootie Williams, Lionel Hampton, and Sonny Greer. When he was not shining shoes, he would leave his post to watch the musicians perform.

However, Malcolm's job did not stop there. He had found a way to supplement his meager pay. Various male guests would approach Malcolm to inquire about buying reefer or meeting prostitutes. Malcolm would provide the guests with the information they wanted and, in return, receive sizable tips. He was able to make a little extra money on the side and continue enjoying the sounds of the big band musicians while working.

Dancing at the Roseland

Malcolm eventually left his shoeshine job to work at a drugstore in Roxbury as a soda fountain boy. There, he earned more money and held a job considered more respectable and prestigious than shining shoes. His sister Ella was delighted, particularly since Malcolm was now working around the children of the middle-class families in Roxbury.Still, Malcolm hadn't lost his love for the swing era music and the nightlife of Roxbury. He continued to frequent the Roseland Ballroom and other dance halls. Wearing his brightly colored zoot suits and shoes, Malcolm became one of the best lindy-hop dancers at the clubs.

At the drugstore, Malcolm was attracted to a quiet, studious girl named Laura. Ella was quite pleased with this news. When Malcolm found out that Laura enjoyed dancing, he invited her out one night to join him at the Roseland Ballroom. Without her strict grandmother's permission, she accepted Malcolm's invitation. That night, Malcolm entered the lindy-hop contest. He did not dance with Laura, however; instead, he chose to dance with another woman at the ballroom who did the lindy hop very well. They did not win the contest, but they were one of the best couples dancing.

Laura was hurt and felt deserted since Malcolm had not chosen her to be his partner. The next time they visited the Roseland Ballroom, she danced much better and Malcolm was very impressed. Unfortunately for Laura, however, this time he was attracted to a well-dressed white woman, Sophia, who had been watching Malcolm and Laura as they danced. He found Sophia so attractive that he hurriedly took Laura home so that he could return to talk with Sophia. After that night, he never dated Laura again. He later learned that Laura had begun drinking and taking drugs, eventually taking up prostitution to support her habits. In his autobiography, Malcolm blamed himself for Laura's downfall.

Malcolm started dating Sophia during an era when interracial relationships were uncommon and were generally frowned upon by society. (In some states at that time, interracial marriage was prohibited by law.) He took pride in having a white girlfriend, since many of his friends saw this as a status symbol. Ella, on the other hand, had liked Laura very much and strongly disapproved of Malcolm dating Sophia. Ella felt that Malcolm had betrayed her trust. Their relationship began to change; eventually Malcolm left Ella's house and moved into an apartment with Shorty. Malcolm was only sixteen, but he was already independent.

Chapter 4

Young Hustler

Malcolm decided to quit his job at the drugstore. He later accepted a better job working as a railroad dishwasher. He was very excited to work for the railroad because he hoped that one day he would get to travel to New York City. At first Malcolm was assigned to a train traveling between Boston and Washington, D.C. After working this route for a few months, he quit. When he started work again for the railroad, he was a sandwich vendor on the Boston-to-New York train. Barely seventeen years old, Malcolm was finally going to explore Harlem, New York.

Harlem

Between his routes, Malcolm would take the subway into Harlem. He was mesmerized by its culture. He visited the club-like restaurant, Small's Paradise, and the Apollo Theater and the Braddock Hotel, where he heard various musicians perform. He would walk to the Savoy Ballroom to watch the big band entertainers and the dancing. The dancing fascinated him more than anything else he had seen in Harlem. The vibrant life of this African-American community had a tremendous impact on young Malcolm.

Soon, however, Malcolm once again quit his railroad job. He decided to return to Lansing to visit his brothers and sisters. Many people he had known in Lansing did not recognize him at first. He had grown much taller, and his hipster, streetwise ways made him appear older than he really was. While there, he visited his mother at the Kalamazoo State Hospital, but she hardly recognized him.

When Malcolm left Michigan, he decided to live in Harlem. The railroad rehired him, but he was fired shortly afterward. He was soon offered a job at Small's Paradise as a waiter. While in Harlem, Malcolm stayed in a building whose tenants included a number of prostitutes. Some of the prostitutes befriended the teenaged Malcolm. They talked with him about sex and other issues related to male-and-female relationships. These women became his substitute mothers.

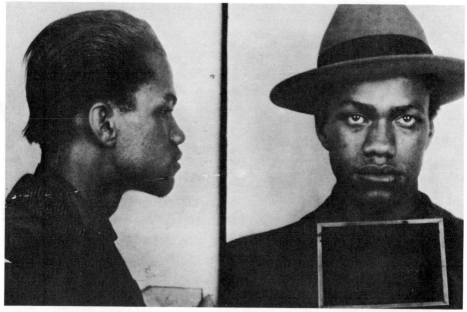

Mug shot of Malcolm X (or Malcolm Little, as he was then named) after his arrest in January, 1946. (Bettmann Archive)

Society of Hustlers

In Harlem, the young Malcolm followed the pattern that had been set in Boston. His role models were not his parents—his father was dead and his mother was in an institution—but rather the male and female hustlers he met during his teen years. These street-hardened figures had a major influence in shaping how Malcolm looked at life and people. Having learned to see life as one big con-game, he had lost respect for people, especially women, and did not really trust anyone.

Working at Small's Paradise did not change Malcolm's role models. At Small's, he met people who hustled to earn money all their lives. There were those who played the illegal numbers game; there were pimps, prostitutes, gamblers, pickpockets, and burglars. Malcolm spent hours listening to the advice of these people, who visited the restaurant frequently. After work, he would visit other bars and sit for hours observing the nightlife of the Harlemites.

At Small's, everyone liked Malcolm. He was a hard worker and willing to learn. When he first took his job, the owner advised Malcolm not to engage in any illegal activities at the restaurant. Malcolm loved his job and obeyed this advice. One day, however, two soldiers asked him about where they could meet some prostitutes. Malcolm quickly gave them the numbers of some of his prostitute friends. It was a decision that he quickly regretted, because he realized they were not soldiers, but undercover policemen.

Malcolm immediately told the manager of his mistake because he knew that the policemen were going to tell the manager anyway. He was hoping that he would be given another chance; instead, he was fired. In order to pay his rent, eat, and get high when he wanted to, Malcolm turned to the streets to hustle full-time.

Going Nowhere

Malcolm met a new friend, Sammy, who taught him how to purchase and sell drugs. Malcolm started selling drugs and earning more money than he ever had. He continued smoking reefer, but he also started using cocaine, heroin, Benzedrine, and whiskey. With more money in his pockets, Malcolm became an addicted gambler, playing the numbers, craps, poker, and other card games for money. He was slowly destroying himself. Malcolm was now pursuing a lifestyle that was sure to result in some kind of tragedy.

In 1943, at the age of eighteen, Malcolm received his draft card to register for the army. Since World War II was then at its height, there was a great likelihood that he would be sent to Europe to fight. This was the last thing that Malcolm wanted to do. To prepare for his pre-induction examination, Malcolm donned his most outrageous outfit. Having entered the recruitment office skipping and talking loudly in hipster slang, he told the army psychiatrist that he could not wait to get his gun so that he could go down South and help kill some of the white people who were causing African Americans to suffer. He was quickly diagnosed as being crazy and was rejected as unfit for service. Malcolm had succeeded in fooling the army.

Malcolm's life became even worse as time went on. He continued selling drugs, but his own drug habit caused him to spend more and more money so that he could stay high. He and Sammy also started robbing stores to get money. When Sammy was shot during one of the robberies, he blamed Malcolm, and this caused their friendship to weaken. Hooked on drugs, unemployed, and constantly threatened with death, Malcolm was relieved when his friend Shorty arrived to take him back to Boston.

In Boston, Malcolm was fortunate to find a job working in a Sears Roebuck Company stock room. He socialized with Shorty and reunited with an old white girlfriend, Bea. Soon, he started missing too many days from work and was fired. Malcolm returned to his life of hustling. He and Shorty, along with Bea and her sister, broke into the houses of well-to-do people when no one was home. After many successful burglaries, Malcolm was finally caught. One day, he took a watch he had stolen to a shop to be repaired. By the time he returned to pick it up, the rightful owner of the watch had been traced. A shocked Malcolm and his friends were immediately arrested for burglary and possession of stolen goods. The fast street life had finally caught up with him.

Chapter 5

Jailbird

Malcolm was convicted of carrying firearms, theft, and breaking and entering. At age twenty-one, he began serving an eight-to-ten-year sentence at the Charlestown Prison outside Boston. When Malcolm entered prison, he quickly earned the nickname "Satan" because he spoke harshly against religion. His fellow prisoners were wary of him, yet they were impressed by his intelligence. Soon, Malcolm became acquainted with another African-American prisoner, nicknamed "Bimbi," who had a great influence on him.

Self-Education

Bimbi was widely respected in prison for his knowledge. Malcolm spent hours talking with him and asking questions. Bimbi encouraged Malcolm to study and take advantage of the prison library. He also suggested that Malcolm enroll in one of the prison correspondence courses. Malcolm enrolled in courses in English and Latin, but primarily he educated himself through intensive reading.

Malcolm was transferred to the Concord Prison Facility in 1947. It was there that he was told about a religion called Islam, which would change his life forever. His brother, Philbert, wrote him and told him about the Nation of Islam. Philbert told Malcolm that Islam was the correct religion for all African Americans. Philbert informed Malcolm that he and several of their siblings had already converted to Islam. Malcolm, however, was still not interested in Islam or any other religion.

Later, another one of Malcolm's brothers, Reginald, wrote

Malcolm to encourage him to stop eating pork and smoking cigarettes. Reginald explained that if Malcolm would stop these two negative habits, it would help him gain his freedom from prison quicker. Reginald told him more about the Nation of Islam and its teachings. White people, he said, far from being superior to blacks, were actually devils, mutants;

Malcolm X in Saudi Arabia with Prince Faisal in 1964. Little did Malcolm realize early in his conversion to Islam, that he would later meet leaders of the world on this road to spiritual understanding. (AP/Wide World Photos)

blackness was the true norm, and whiteness a deviation from it. Malcolm was shocked to learn such news. He stopped eating pork, as Reginald had urged, and befriended another prisoner who was already a member of the Nation of Islam. They spent hours talking together. Malcolm was slowly becoming interested in Islam.

Later that same year, Malcolm was transferred to the Norfolk Prison Colony. Norfolk accepted only the best-behaved prisoners. There, they had greater freedom and more privileges. Norfolk had dormitories, a nice recreation room, showers, and an excellent library. Malcolm studied whenever he had free time, even at night when the lighting was very poor. Eventually he had to wear glasses. The first book Malcolm studied was the dictionary. To improve his vocabulary and writing style, he worked his way through the entire dictionary, carefully studying the definitions of every word from A to Z.

When his brother Reginald visited, Malcolm was anxious to learn more about the Nation of Islam. His other brothers and sisters wrote him more often to encourage him to join the Nation. When his sister Hilda visited him, this had an even greater impact on him. Before leaving, she suggested that Malcolm write directly to Elijah Muhammad himself, the leader of the Nation of Islam. Malcolm took her advice, and he was quite pleased when Muhammad answered his letters each time he wrote.

Conversion

Malcolm finally decided to join the Nation of Islam. He became a devout Muslim and changed his lifestyle completely. Even before his conversion he had transformed himself into a bookworm. History, philosophy, literature, psychology, economics, religion: All of these subjects absorbed him. When he was not reading, he would share what he learned with his prison friends. He joined the Norfolk prison debating team and became an outstanding debater.

For the first time since his eighth-grade teacher discouraged him from becoming a lawyer, Malcolm felt like an intelligent person who could accomplish anything that he wanted to do.

He was successful in recruiting a few other prisoners to join the Nation of Islam. He was later transferred back to the Charlestown Prison, where he continued to recruit fellow inmates into the Nation. In 1952, after more than six years in prison, Malcolm was released on parole. Now, he had the freedom to learn more about his new religion.

Chapter 6

The Nation of Islam

Malcolm had read that Islam was founded in the seventh century in Arabia by a prophet named Muhammad in a city called Mecca. To many African Americans, as to most other Americans, Islam was a foreign religion about which they knew very little and with which they felt no connection. Yet to the small group of African Americans whom Malcolm had joined, Islam was a lost birthright which they were determined to reclaim, a vital link to their African homeland.

Founded in Detroit around 1930, the Nation of Islam combined orthodox Muslim doctrines with teachings of its own (see page 29). Members of the Nation of Islam, or Black Muslims, were taught that African Americans are lost descendants of African Muslims. (In fact, most African Americans have their roots in non-Muslim regions of Africa, where various African religions predominated.)

Black Muslims also had distinctive beliefs about racial differences. When Malcolm's sister, Hilda, visited him in prison, she told him about the origins of white people. Members of the Nation of Islam believed that whites were created by an angry scientist named Yacub who wanted to get revenge for being expelled from his society. Yacub, therefore, created white people to spread confusion and destruction among black people in the world everywhere. The Nation of Islam sought to prepare African Americans for judgment day, when the good forces of black people would defeat the evil forces of white people.

These teachings were a mirror-image of the distorted racial attitudes of the white majority. Many white people believed that black people were inferior by nature. Day after day, in thousands of ways, society reinforced the message that white was better than black. The Black Muslims took this message and reversed it.

The Black Muslims encouraged African Americans to love themselves more. The Nation of Islam taught African history to its members so that they would be proud of their heritage. This black nationalist organization believed in hard work, cleanliness, obeying the law, and staying separate from white people. Sexual promiscuity and the use of drugs, alcohol, and tobacco were strictly forbidden. The Nation of Islam also encouraged economic independence and opened businesses, such as restaurants, bakeries, and grocery stores, in African-American communities.

Elijah Muhammad, leader of the Nation of Islam (NOI) from 1934 until his death in 1975. (Roy Lewis Photography)

Meeting Elijah Muhammad

Elijah Muhammad, whom Malcolm had corresponded with while serving his prison sentence, had been leading the Nation of Islam since 1934. Known to his followers as the Honorable Prophet Elijah Muhammad, Elijah Muhammad was called Elijah Poole at birth. He was the son of a Georgia Baptist

The 12 Points of Elijah Muhammad

1. *Separate from the slave master.*

2. *Pool your resources, education, and qualifications for independence.*

3. *Stop forcing yourself into places where you are not wanted.*

4. *Make your neighborhood a decent place to live in.*

5. *Rid yourself of the lust for wine and drink.*

6. *Learn to love self and kind before loving others.*

7. *Unite to create a future for yourself.*

8. *Build your own schools, hospitals, factories.*

9. *Do not seek to mix your blood through racial integration.*

10. *Stop buying expensive cars, fine clothes, and shoes before being able to live in a fine home.*

11. *Spend your money among yourselves.*

12. *Protect your women.*

Mecca, Saudi Arabia, the birthplace of Muhammad, to which all devout Muslims make a pilgrimage. (AP/Wide World Photos)

preacher who relocated the family to Detroit in the 1920's. Like Malcolm's parents and many other African Americans, the Pooles were disappointed by what they found in the North, where only the lowest-paying jobs were available to them. They learned, too, that racial prejudice was not confined to the South.

Still searching for solutions, some of these disenchanted African Americans turned to the Nation of Islam. Among them was Elijah Poole. Under his leadership as Elijah Muhammad, the Nation of Islam began to grow, though still only a very small percentage of African Americans became members of the Nation of Islam.

Now that Malcolm had become a Muslim, he looked forward to one day seeing the man whose influence had helped to change his life. First, however, he wanted to visit his mother in Kalamazoo. Their meeting in the hospital was very painful for him; she did not recognize him at all.

Malcolm stayed with his brother Wilfred in Detroit and worked in his brother's furniture store as a salesman. He later worked in a factory that paid more money. He attended the Muslims' Temple Number One in Detroit. One day, the members were all driving to Chicago to hear Elijah Muhammad speak at Temple Number Two. Malcolm was excited because, for the first time, he would get to see the Prophet Elijah Muhammad. After his speech, Muhammad invited Malcolm and his family to his home for dinner. This was an honor that Malcolm had never dreamed of having.

X

Names are not merely labels. They are chosen with care, and they have great symbolic value. Members of the Nation of Islam believed that African Americans should not use the family names that had been given to their ancestors by their white slavemasters. To symbolize their rejection of slavery and of white American culture, some Black Muslims replaced their family names with an "X," which represented the lost African names of their ancestors. Shortly after his visit to Chicago, Malcolm received his X for his dedicated, hard work: Malcolm Little had become Malcolm X.

Impressed with the large membership of Temple Number Two, Malcolm questioned Muhammad about what he could do to build the membership of Detroit's Temple Number One. Muhammad advised him to recruit more young people. When Malcolm returned to Detroit, he worked very hard to recruit young members. He traveled around Detroit and also began visiting other surrounding cities and towns. Malcolm now was

Islam and the Nation of Islam

Muhammad was born in A.D. 570 in the city of Mecca, in what is today Saudi Arabia. He experienced poverty and misfortune in his early life; as he grew older, he became keenly aware of problems that troubled his society. In 610, he heard a voice telling him that he was to be the messenger for God, or Allah. Thus Muhammad began his career as an apostle for Allah, spreading a new religion called Islam. He wrote down messages believed to have come directly from God, compiling them in the holy book known as the Qu'ran or Koran.

Muhammad and his followers, called Muslims, sought improvement of the relationship between people and God. They also wanted to improve human relationships in society. Muslims were expected to spread the Islamic value system of obedience, faithfulness, and cleanliness throughout the world—by conquest, if necessary.

In the centuries after Muhammad laid these foundations, Islam did indeed spread rapidly, not only in the Middle East but also in Asia and Africa. By the 16th century, Islamic armies were poised to conquer Europe, but military defeats and internal weaknesses of the Islamic empires halted their progress. From its humble beginnings, Islam had developed into a great world religion with a rich civilization. People of many different races and cultures shared a common identity as Muslims, belonging to one community and having one faith.

The precise origins of the Black Muslim movement in the United States are not certain. Some scholars trace its beginnings to the forming of the Moorish Science Temple by Prophet (Timothy) Drew Ali in Newark, N.J., in 1913. It is generally agreed, however, that the movement did not begin to grow until the 1930's, under the leadership of Wallace D. Fard Muhammad (or Wali Fard), an orthodox Muslim who had immigrated to the United States from the Middle East.

First active in Detroit around 1930, Fard established a temple and a school there. Heavily influenced by Marcus Garvey's UNIA, which advocated black nationalism and black separatism, Fard preached these same principles to his early followers.

After Fard's disappearance in 1934, Elijah Muhammad took his place, and under his direction the organization became known as the Nation of Islam. The Nation of Islam came to national prominence in the late 1950's through the speeches of its most charismatic personality, Malcolm X.

Under Elijah Muhammad, the Nation of Islam preached that peoples of African descent were culturally and morally superior to white people. The Black Muslims encouraged African Americans to stop practicing Christianity, since it was the religion of a white race of devils whose sole purpose was to rule over black people and make them suffer. The Nation of Islam believed in black separatism and wanted African Americans to be given certain states so that they could establish their own country within the United States. The worldwide Islamic community did not recognize the members of the Nation of Islam as being true Muslims, because they excluded people from other races and preached black supremacy.

spreading the teachings of Elijah Muhammad, just as his own father had done thirty years earlier with the teachings of Marcus Garvey.

Malcolm's work paid off as the membership of Temple Number One grew larger. Because of Malcolm's dedicated work in building the Nation of Islam, he was made the assistant minister of the Temple. Elijah Muhammad was very impressed. He encouraged Malcolm to visit the Chicago Temple more often so that they could talk. Malcolm accepted the invitation, and he and Muhammad began to develop a father-son relationship. Malcolm felt that he had found the father that he had long been missing.

Malcolm had the privilege of learning the teachings of Islam directly from the Nation's prophet. He stayed in Chicago for a while with Muhammad and was trained to become a minister. Malcolm grew to become one of Muhammad's most committed followers. He quit his factory job and became a full-time organizer for the Nation of Islam.

Muhammad instructed Malcolm to relocate to Boston and develop a Nation of Islam chapter there. Malcolm returned to Boston in 1953. He encouraged his African-American audiences to work hard and be very disciplined in whatever they did. Within three months, Malcolm had successfully established a Temple in Boston. He placed Minister Louis X, later called Louis Farrakhan, in charge and then left to become the Acting Minister of the Temple in Philadelphia.

Malcolm's popularity in the Nation was beginning to grow. The skills he had developed while debating in prison made him the most effective speaker in the Nation of Islam. In 1954, after Malcolm's success in Detroit, Boston, and Philadelphia, Muhammad appointed Malcolm as Minister of Temple Number Seven, in New York City. For the first time since his hustler days, Malcolm was going to return to his beloved Harlem.

Chapter 7

Minister Malcolm

It was in Harlem that Malcolm had sunk to the life of dishonesty, drug abuse, and crime that almost destroyed him. In 1954, he was in Harlem again—a new man with a new mission. He was determined to be a successful Minister in Temple Number Seven. Within ten years of his arrival, the name Malcolm X was known not only in Harlem but also throughout the United States and around the world.

When Malcolm first arrived in Harlem, he wanted to see some of his old acquaintances and visit some of the places he had once known. At first, few people recognized him. Once again Malcolm's appearance had changed dramatically; the flamboyant zoot-suit-wearing hustler with conked hair had been transformed to a clean-cut man in a conservative suit, with glasses that gave him a scholarly look and short natural hair. Many of his acquaintances were either dead, badly hooked on drugs, or in poor health. Drugs, prostitution, pimping, poor housing, and hustling were still present everywhere. Harlem had changed very little since Malcolm last saw it.

Building the Nation

Temple Number Seven had a small membership. Malcolm and his assistants began passing out flyers to people on the streets telling them about the meetings at Temple Number Seven. They would pass them out to people leaving the various black nationalist meetings and to others coming from church. Once people came, Malcolm was careful of what he said to his audience, since most of them had not heard the teachings of

Elijah Muhammad before. He knew how to talk to them and help them understand these new ideas of Elijah Muhammad. Slowly, the membership of Temple Number Seven began to grow.

While he worked in Harlem, and organized Temples elsewhere in New York City, in Brooklyn and Queens, Malcolm was still responsible for the Temples in Boston and Philadelphia. He also helped to organize new Temples in Springfield, Massachusetts and Hartford, Connecticut. He actively helped to build the Nation of Islam by further organizing Temples in upstate New York, New Jersey, Pennsylvania, Florida, Ohio, and Virginia. By 1956, the membership of the Nation of Islam—while still very small in comparison to Christian denominations—had increased significantly, numbering in the tens of thousands. Elijah Muhammad could not have been prouder of the efforts of his prize student.

Malcolm worked very hard. He spent long, late hours in Temple Number Seven holding special classes for the Fruit of Islam (the paramilitary wing of the Nation of Islam), the Muslim Girls Training Night, Unity Night, and, on Friday nights, the General Civilization study sessions. Then, on Sundays, he preached at the early afternoon services.

The Hinton Incident

Malcolm had risen to become the top organizer for the Nation of Islam. One event in particular illustrated the growing popularity of Malcolm and the respect African Americans had for him. In New York in 1957, a Black Muslim observed some policemen beating a drunken man. When the Muslim bystander, a man named Johnson Hinton, protested loudly against what he saw as police brutality, he too was beaten and arrested. As soon as some other Muslims found out about the incident, they gathered in large numbers outside the precinct

Malcolm X at an NOI rally in 1963; he and Louis Lomax founded the newspaper Muham-mad Speaks *in 1957.* (AP/Wide World Photos)

station, demanding Hinton's release.

When Malcolm arrived, he was not allowed to visit Hinton. He quickly warned the police that the Muslims assembled outside would not leave until he was able to check the condition of his fellow believer. By this time, the crowd had increased from a few hundred to thousands. Both Muslims and other people from the larger community heard of the event and had gathered to lend support or just out of curiosity. Because of the potential for a riot, the police decided to permit Malcolm to visit Hinton.

Malcolm made certain that Hinton received proper medical care. He then demanded that the officers involved in the incident be investigated and punished. Afterward, Malcolm went outside to the restless crowd. He motioned for the people to disperse, and the huge crowd retreated peacefully and cleared the streets. Upon observing this, one white official remarked that "no black man should have that much power."

Spellbinding Speeches

It was obvious that Malcolm had become an important and influential leader in the African-American community. The Hinton incident not only increased the growing popularity of Malcolm X but also increased the popularity of the Nation of Islam. The New York City police and the Federal Bureau of Investigation (FBI) quickly sought more information about this influential young leader.

On many occasions, Malcolm was called upon to introduce Elijah Muhammad to an audience. He would give short, emotional speeches filled with both facts and humorous stories that would warm the audience up for the main speaker. On other occasions, when Malcolm himself was the featured speaker, the auditoriums were packed with people, standing-room only. As Malcolm did for Muhammad, Minister Louis X would warm up the audience and introduce Malcolm.

...by any means necessary

Distributed by Young Socialist Alliance
P.O. Box 471, Cooper Station, N.Y., N.Y. 10003

1. Poster depicting Malcolm X and one of his more controversial statements. (Library of Congress)

John Launois, Black Star

3. Martin Luther King, Jr. (AP/Wide World Photos)

4. A billboard for Spike Lee's 1992 film, *Malcolm X*. (Frances M. Roberts)

November

5. Malcolm X's widow, Betty Shabazz, holding a copy of his autobiography. (Frances M. Roberts)

6. John F. Kennedy, the thirty-fifth president of the United States. (AP/Wide World Photos)

7. Malcolm X Boulevard in New York City. (Batt Johnson, Unicorn Stock Photos)

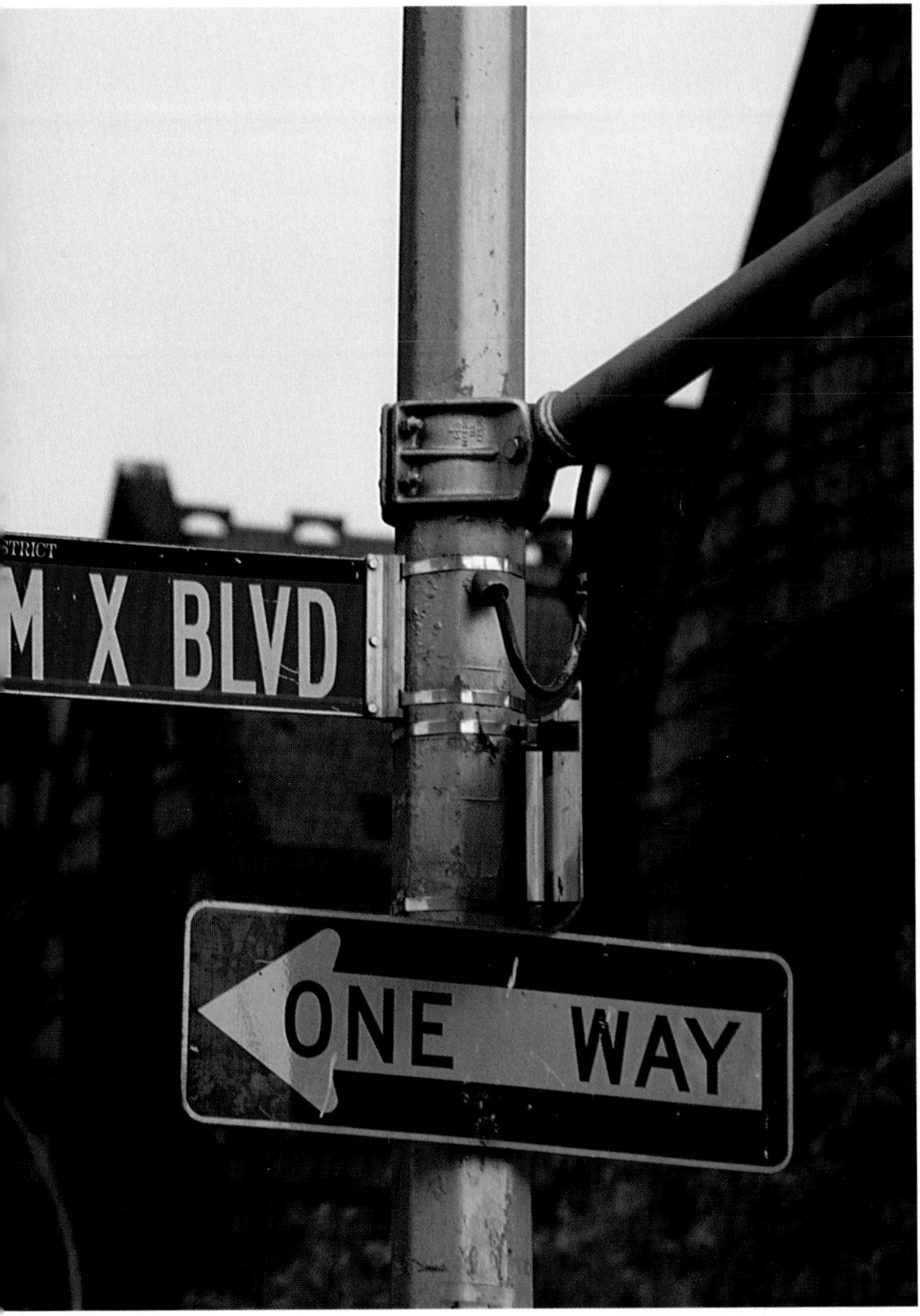
STRICT
M X BLVD
ONE WAY

8. A thoughtful moment while visiting Mecca. (John Launois, Black Star)

9. African American man wearing a Malcolm X t-shirt, symbolizing both a pride in a shared heritage and the extent to which the ideas that Malcolm X represented have become a part of the popular culture. (Robert W. Ginn, Unicorn Stock Photos)

10. Malcolm X as part of a black history and pride poster. (Batt Johnson, Unicorn Stock Photos)

11. A plea for racial harmony after the 1992 Los Angeles riots. (AP/Wide World Photos)

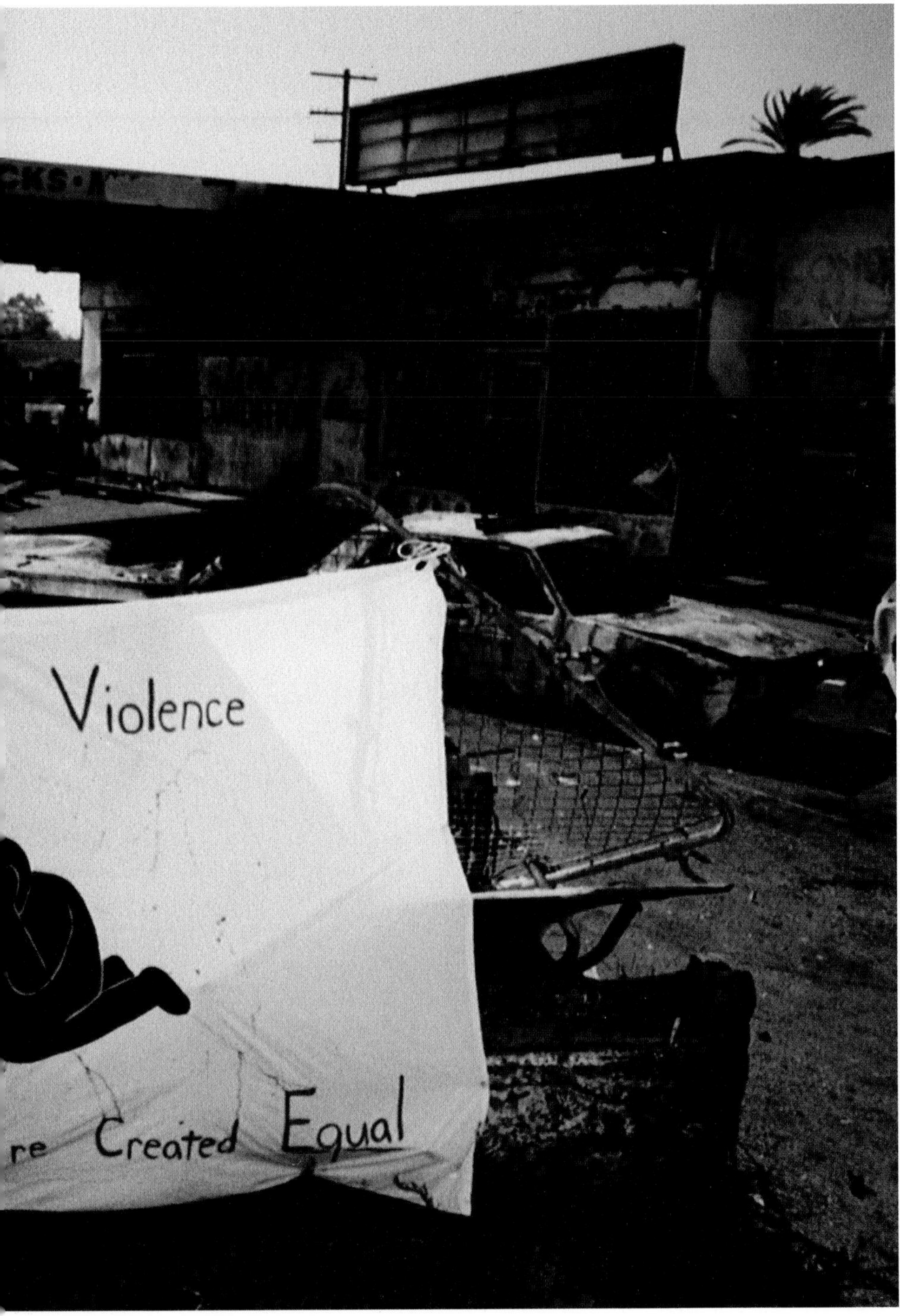
Violence
re Created Equal

Malcolm's eloquent speaking style would hold his audiences' attention for hours.

One reason that Malcolm was so successful as a speaker was that he adapted his style and his message to the particular audience he was addressing. In the same week, he might speak to an all-white audience of college students and an audience of poor, uneducated African Americans on the street corners of Harlem. His speeches ranged from scholarly discussions of history and science to the mythical theories taught by Elijah Muhammad.

One theory, in particular, that Malcolm strongly believed in and enjoyed delivering to his African-American audience was the Yacub theory. In fact, he had become the best speaker in the Nation of Islam to explain why white people were nothing but "blonde-haired, blue-eyed devils" and African Americans, on the other hand, were the superior race. The Yacub philosophy quickly earned the Nation of Islam and Malcolm the label of being "hatemongers"—people who preached hatred.

In 1957, Elijah Muhammad appointed Malcolm X as his National Representative. Malcolm continued to work very hard and usually slept no more than three or four hours a night. He was constantly traveling, attending meetings, and talking on the telephone. At times, he worked twenty-four hours at a stretch to complete an important job. Later that same year, Malcolm, with the assistance of Louis Lomax, started a newspaper, *Muhammad Speaks*, that became one of the most influential voices in the African-American community. Malcolm worshipped Elijah Muhammad and was deeply committed to building the Nation of Islam.

Marriage and Family

In spite of his busy life, Malcolm was interested in settling down and having a family. In 1958, he was attracted to a

college student, Betty Sanders, who came to New York City
from Tuskegee Institute in Alabama to attend nursing school.
Betty attended one of Malcolm's lectures at Temple Number
Seven and was impressed with his clean-cut appearance and
no-nonsense attitude. She was introduced to him after the
lecture and he immediately invited her to visit again.

Betty attended a few more lectures at the Temple and later
joined the Nation of Islam. She and Malcolm became friends,
but the Nation of Islam did not permit males and females to
socialize freely together at the Temple. Therefore, whenever
Malcolm had free time in the midst of his busy schedule, he
would take Betty to dinner or talk with her after his lectures.

While away on a trip to Detroit, Malcolm called Betty and
surprised her by asking to marry her. She happily said yes and
met him the next day in Detroit, where her parents lived. After
Malcolm was introduced to her parents, the two drove to
Lansing, where Malcolm's family lived, to marry. After their
return to New York, the Nation of Islam provided the couple
with a nice house in Queens, New York. They eventually had
six daughters (the last two of whom, twins, Malcolm didn't
live to see; they were born several months after his
assassination). Even though his job often took him away from
home, when there Malcolm loved being a father and a family
man.

By Any Means Necessary

Malcolm continued to be an effective spokesperson for the
Nation of Islam. He traveled abroad to the Netherlands, the
Middle East, and Africa as the Nation of Islam's ambassador.
He was a delightful speaker, and his growing popularity was
sometimes envied by others, including his fellow Muslims.

Because he was both articulate and provocative, Malcolm
was often contacted by the media. He appeared on television
and radio talk shows representing the Nation of Islam and was

The 1963 March on Washington. (AP/Wide World Photos)

frequently written about or interviewed in magazines and newspapers. The media had become more interested in Malcolm than they were in his leader, Elijah Muhammad. In spite of his growing popularity, in every speech or interview Malcolm always referred to the teachings of the "Honorable Elijah Muhammad" and repeatedly credited Muhammad for everything he had accomplished.

Malcolm's knowledge of history and his awareness of the various political events affecting African Americans were evident in his speeches. His wit and wisdom continued to hypnotize his audiences. Malcolm was not afraid to speak up and criticize the ill-treatment and discrimination which African

Americans had suffered and continued to suffer.

The Nation of Islam prohibited its members from participating in the integrated Civil Rights movement headed by such leaders as Dr. Martin Luther King, Jr., Ralph Abernathy, Roy Wilkins, and others. Strongly opposed to any form of integration, the Black Muslims believed in the complete separation of the races. For many years, no whites had been admitted into the Nation's Temples; later, white reporters were allowed to attend select events.

The Nation of Islam believed that the Civil Rights movement should not have been an integrated movement of African-American and white activists, but only of African Americans. While King and other Civil Rights leaders were striving for a color-blind society, in which African Americans and whites could attend the same schools and use the same public facilities, Malcolm was sarcastically describing the Civil Rights movement as a fight for the right "to sit next to a white person on the toilet." He harshly dismissed the 1963 March on Washington, in which more than 200,000 people assembled to protest racial discrimination, as a circus led by "Uncle Tom" African-American leaders.

The Nation of Islam also disagreed with King's philosophy of nonviolence. King's nonviolent philosophy, based in part on the teachings of Gandhi and in part on his Christian heritage, called for people to avoid physical resistance or violence, even when they were being beaten or spat on by whites, bitten by dogs, or knocked down by powerful water hoses. The Nation of Islam, on the other hand, endorsed the philosophy of "an eye for an eye and a tooth for a tooth." Black Muslims believed that if someone was being physically abused, he had the right to defend himself.

In his speeches, Malcolm stressed that the Muslims would not tolerate the kind of abuse that was accepted by nonviolent Civil Rights demonstrators in the South. He warned that

Malcolm X in Washington, D.C., in 1963. (AP/Wide World Photos)

Muslims would defend themselves against violence "by any means necessary." He added that violence could only be defeated with violence, not a "turn the other cheek" philosophy that he attributed the the nonviolent movement.

Malcolm pointed out that the basic principles of freedom, justice, and equality on which the United States had been founded had never applied to its African-American citizens. He was very critical of the policies of President John Kennedy and, later, President Lyndon Johnson. He spoke out against the United States' role in the Vietnam War and against European colonization in Africa.

Within the Civil Rights movement, African-American students were slowly being influenced by the words and ideas of Malcolm X. Many of them began to agree with the black nationalist teachings of the Nation of Islam as expressed by Malcolm. Even though Black Muslims were not supposed to be involved with the Civil Rights movement, Malcolm was indirectly involved since his ideas were influencing those in the movement.

Malcolm still looked to Elijah Muhammad for guidance and respected him as a son to a father. He publicly credited the "Prophet Muhammad" with transforming his life. He had complete faith in Muhammad's teachings and daily practices. Malcolm himself lived a very moral and simple lifestyle. He was critical of any incidents of infidelity, mishandling of money, and other forms of dishonesty or misconduct in the Nation of Islam.

Conflict with Elijah Muhammad

As Malcolm's popularity increased both inside and outside the Nation of Islam, personal jealousies emerged within the organization. Some Muslims became critical of Malcolm's prominence, suggesting that he was overshadowing Elijah Muhammad. As a result, Malcolm began to refuse speaking engagements or interviews and continued to express his loyalty to Muhammad.

In the early 1960's, however, political differences and other problems slowly emerged to divide Malcolm and Muhammad. Muhammad was critical of Malcolm's fiery speaking style and suggested that Malcolm tone his speeches down so that they would not invite controversy. He also criticized Malcolm for his growing interest and minor involvement in the Civil Rights movement. On several occasions, Malcolm had participated in local rallies or demonstrations.

Malcolm urged Muhammad to abandon the policy of nonparticipation in politics. More important, Malcolm began to question some of the fundamental teachings of Elijah Muhammad, particularly the mythical theories pertaining to the evolution of whites. Was it really true that all whites were evil, and that they all despised people of African descent?

At the same time, Malcolm began to have doubts about Elijah Muhammad's personal conduct. Earlier, when he had heard rumors that Muhammad had several girlfriends who had borne his children, Malcolm had ignored the charges, calling them malicious gossip. In 1962, however, he learned that the rumors were true. His beloved Elijah Muhammad had been unfaithful to his wife and had gotten several young female members in the Nation of Islam pregnant. Moreover, Muhammad refused to take financial responsibility for the illegitimate children he had fathered.

When Malcolm learned of this news, he felt that his world had come to an end. He had spent a major part of his adult years carrying out the work of a man he admired and respected. For the first time since he had joined the Nation of Islam, he felt betrayed. Still, Malcolm did not want the public to know of these affairs. He knew that such information could ruin the Nation of Islam.

After this point, there was much tension and distrust

71

between the two men. Muhammad and others began to suggest that Malcolm was interested in taking over the leadership of the Nation of Islam. Malcolm, in the meantime, was still trying to recover from the shocking revelation of Muhammad's hypocrisy and deceitfulness.

At the same time, Malcolm was becoming more critical of the mishandling of money in the Nation of Islam and the extravagant lifestyles of some Muslims. While Malcolm lived a life of austerity in a house owned by the Nation of Islam, Elijah Muhammad and his children lived in luxurious homes. Profits from the businesses owned by the Nation of Islam largely benefitted Muhammad's family. These differences and criticisms led to the gradual deterioration of the relationship between Malcolm and Muhammad.

Chapter 8

Suspended

President John F. Kennedy was in office during some of the key events of the Civil Rights movement. His presidential campaign had included promises to end racial discrimination in the United States. Once in office, however, he did not move quickly to carry out his promises. Even when peaceful Civil Rights demonstrators in the South were being beaten and harassed by policemen and white mobs, the federal government did little to protect the demonstrators against the brutality and abuse. As a result, the Kennedy Administration received criticism from the Civil Rights movement.

The Nation of Islam was also critical of the Kennedy Administration. Malcolm X was particularly relentless in his attacks. He told his audiences that Kennedy was no more a friend to African Americans than was the Ku Klux Klan or the well-known Southern segregationists, George Wallace of Alabama and Ross Barnett of Mississippi. Nevertheless, when Kennedy was assassinated in November, 1963, Elijah Muhammad instructed his ministers not to make any comments about the president's death. Muhammad believed that, at a time when the nation was mourning, any negative comments about Kennedy might damage the public image of the Nation of Islam.

Nine days after the assassination, Malcolm X spoke before an audience in New York City. During the question-and-answer segment, Malcolm was asked about Kennedy's death. Malcolm observed that Kennedy "never foresaw that the chickens would come home to roost so soon." Since Kennedy's Administration had not acted decisively to stop the violence against African Americans that existed in the South, Malcolm saw Kennedy himself as a victim of the violence he tolerated in his own country.

Malcolm X with Muhammad Ali (formerly Cassius Clay), in 1964, shortly after the new heavyweight champion announced his conversion to Islam. (AP/Wide World Photos)

Breaking with the Nation

Malcolm had directly disobeyed Muhammad's orders by commenting on the late president's death. A few days later, Muhammad informed Malcolm that his comments had hurt the Nation of Islam. As a result, he forbade Malcolm to speak publicly for ninety days. Silencing Malcolm prohibited him from being the Nation of Islam's spokesperson. It also interfered with Malcolm's investigation of Elijah Muhammad's immoral conduct, since other Muslims were not allowed to communicate with him.

When the press questioned Malcolm, he politely informed them that he had been suspended from public speaking and would obey the Honorable Elijah Muhammad's orders. In January, 1964, Elijah Muhammad told Malcolm that he was no longer the National Representative for the Nation of Islam nor the Minister of Harlem's Temple Number Seven, now called Mosque Number Seven. Malcolm was deeply hurt and depressed over his demotion in the Nation. Even more hurtful was the reaction of some of his fellow Muslims, who suddenly began to treat him as a nonperson and refused to speak to him. Furthermore, Muhammad demanded that Malcolm and his family move out of their home in Queens, since that house belonged to the Nation of Islam.

Malcolm relied on his wife, Betty, for comfort. She was very supportive of her husband. He knew that the gap between himself and Elijah Muhammad had widened even deeper. Malcolm was now under a great deal of stress. He felt the need to escape at least briefly from the pressures of New York. He had been interested in boxing since his boyhood days, and he welcomed an invitation from the boxer Cassius Clay to visit his training camp in Miami, Florida. Clay was preparing to fight the heavyweight champion, Sonny Liston, and wanted Malcolm there to serve as his spiritual advisor. It was after this fight that Clay announced his conversion to Islam and his

Martin Luther King, Jr., and Malcolm X in Washington, D.C., March, 1964—their only face to face meeting. (AP/Wide World Photos)

membership in the Nation of Islam; thereafter he was known by his Islamic name, Muhammad Ali.

During this trip, Malcolm realized that Elijah Muhammad had no intention of reinstating him in the Nation of Islam. Malcolm also began receiving death threats from other Black Muslims. Malcolm realized that his membership in the Nation was over.

A New Direction

In March, 1964, Malcolm held two press conferences in New York City to inform the public of his break with the Nation of Islam. At one conference, he announced that he was going to become an active participant in the Civil Rights movement. At the second conference, he announced the formation of a new Muslim organization, the Muslim Mosque, Inc.

Malcolm's public rallies after his break with the Nation of Islam addressed the need for African Americans to gain political power. He became much less critical of other African-American leaders; he wanted to work with them to bring about equality for his people. For the first and only time, he met Martin Luther King, Jr., face-to-face, in Washington, D.C., at some congressional hearings on civil rights legislation.

It was during this period of change that Malcolm decided he wanted to take a trip to Mecca, the Islamic holy city in Saudi Arabia. This pilgrimage, called the *hajj*, was one that every devout Muslim hoped to make at least once. Malcolm had traveled to the Middle East previously, when he was in the Nation of Islam. However, illness had prevented him from visiting the holy city. This time, he was determined to make the trip. After getting the necessary papers, he visited his sister Ella in Boston to borrow money for the journey.

Ella had also left the Nation of Islam and was now studying orthodox Islam. Financially comfortable as a result of her earnings from real estate, she, too, was planning a trip to Mecca, but she immediately gave Malcolm the money he needed to take the trip instead. In April, 1964, Malcolm was on his way.

Chapter 9

Genesis

The first Muslim city Malcolm visited was Cairo, Egypt. There, he spent two days sightseeing. From Cairo, he traveled to Jedda, Saudi Arabia. Malcolm was not allowed to travel further to his destination, Mecca, until his paperwork was confirmed. During this delay, he was able to review his life and his ideas as a Black Muslim in the United States. In the Middle East, Malcolm was surrounded by non-black Muslims who treated him equally, as a brother. On his journey, he did not experience racial discrimination in any form.

Malcolm saw clearly that white people were not a devil-race. He realized that the teachings of Elijah Muhammad were wrong. He knew now that not all whites were racists, and that even white people could be Muslims.

Malcolm X was made a guest of the state in Saudi Arabia. He had never felt so special. He was being welcomed with great respect by white-skinned people. He wrote of his wonderfully shocking experiences in many letters back to the United States. He wanted everyone to know of his discoveries and his decision to embrace orthodox Islam.

Africa

Malcolm's trip to Mecca was followed by a three-week tour of Africa. In May, he traveled back to Egypt and then on to Nigeria in West Africa. In Nigeria, he was interviewed on both radio and television. He later addressed a standing-room-only audience at the University of Ibadan. The Nigerian students proudly named him *Omawali*, a Yoruba word meaning "child who returns home."

Malcolm X in Egypt meeting with Palestinian leader Ahmed Shukairi in 1964. (AP/Wide World Photos)

Next, Malcolm visited Ghana. Again, he received a warm welcome and was treated with the respect usually reserved for heads of state. There, he met President Osagyefo Kwame Nkrumah, who had a great impact on Malcolm's thinking. Nkrumah was one of the leading advocates of pan-Africanism, the belief that all African people—and people of African descent worldwide—should recognize their shared identity and strive to achieve common goals. Malcolm also met W. E. B. Du Bois' widow, Shirley Graham Du Bois, who had relocated to Ghana several years earlier with her late husband. From Ghana, Malcolm traveled to Liberia, Senegal, Morocco, and Algeria.

While on this journey, Malcolm adopted the name El-Hajj Malik El-Shabazz to signify that he had taken the *hajj* and to symbolize his adherence to orthodox Islam. However, he continued to use the name Malcolm X as well. In May of 1964, he arrived back in New York City.

The Organization of African-American Unity

In New York, Malcolm faced his largest press conference concerning his travels abroad. He told of his experiences and admitted that he had made mistakes in the past when he generalized about white people. He confessed that he had learned that white people were not devils and that not all whites were racists. He told of his surprise at seeing Muslims who were white and described how he had prayed and slept side-by-side with them, without feeling any discrimination.

Malcolm announced that his organization, Muslim Mosque, Inc., would not follow the teachings of Elijah Muhammad. Instead, it would practice the true, orthodox Islam. Malcolm, a more relaxed man with a new worldview, set out to build a Muslim temple or mosque centered on the Islamic philosophy followed by the millions of Muslims in Africa, Asia, and the Middle East.

In June, Malcolm established another organization, called the Organization of Afro-American Unity (OAAU). This pan-African organization, modeled after Marcus Garvey's UNIA and Africa's Organization of African Unity (OAU), was a nonreligious political organization. It was a black nationalist organization that accepted all African Americans and people of African descent who wanted to fight for the civil rights and human rights of African Americans. OAAU members included some of the more militant African-American activists, and, in contrast to the Nation of Islam, many of its members and chief organizers were women.

Even though Malcolm no longer believed that whites were inherently evil, he never became an integrationist. He was still a committed black nationalist who believed in African Americans working together to solve their own problems. He remained suspicious of most whites in the United States, who were very different from the whites he had met on his travels in the Middle East and Africa. In fact, it was these travels that convinced Malcolm of the need for all black people to unite and fight for human rights for African Americans in the United States. He saw that such a fight would involve the international community and should be brought before the United Nations.

Denounced by the Nation of Islam

The major split within the Nation of Islam had become public. Malcolm wrote a letter to Elijah Muhammad and had it published in a New York newspaper. Even though the conflict between the two men was severe, Malcolm made an effort to overcome their differences, but Muhammad was not interested in reconciliation.

Muhammad and other Muslims, including Minister Louis X, who at one time had served as Malcolm's assistant minister, continued to write articles in the newspaper *Muhammad Speaks* denouncing Malcolm, creating a climate of hate toward

Malcolm in the Nation of Islam. In the meantime, the women who had borne Elijah Muhammad's children out of wedlock continued to sue him for child support. Other Nation of Islam members and relatives of Muhammad, including two of his

Malcolm X in Tanganyika with Abdul Rahman Babu, minister of state of the United Republic of Tanganyika and Zanzibar. (AP/Wide World Photos)

sons, Wallace and Akbar, eventually resigned as a result of their disagreement with his teachings and his immoral activities.

Return to Africa

In July, 1964, Malcolm returned to Africa and stayed for

four months, visiting different countries. He first attended the OAU conference in Cairo, Egypt. Even though he did not represent an African country, he was allowed to attend as a delegate. He circulated a petition urging OAU members to bring the issue of American racism and discrimination against African Americans before the United Nations. Malcolm wanted to internationalize the African-American struggle by connecting the problems of his people to the problems of the larger black community throughout the world. This was one of Malcolm's most important pan-African activities.

When Malcolm left Cairo, he traveled for two months throughout Africa. During this visit and his previous visit to Africa, he had the opportunity to meet many African leaders. By the middle of October, Malcolm had visited eleven African countries, talked with their heads of state, and even addressed their parliaments.

Within a few weeks after returning to New York in November, Malcolm left again to travel abroad. This time he went to London to participate in a debate at Oxford University, where he argued that if nonviolence failed to gain freedom and equality for African Americans, then violence was necessary. Afterward, he spoke at different functions in the United States, including an event at the Harvard University Law School. Throughout his travels in the United States and abroad, the FBI and the Central Intelligence Agency (CIA) closely monitored Malcolm's activities.

Tensions still existed between the Nation of Islam and the Muslims who had left the organization. Threats were being made not only against Malcolm's life but also against the lives of other dissident Black Muslims. The Nation of Islam continued court proceedings to evict Malcolm's family from their house. On the other hand, increasing numbers of Muslims who had left the Nation spoke out against the organization for distorting Islam and teaching racial hatred.

84

Besides trying to build the Muslim Mosque and the OAAU in Harlem, Malcolm was still traveling to speak at various engagements in and out of the country. He lectured to college students and continued to criticize the nonviolent methods advocated by the leaders of the Civil Rights movement. He called for black nationalism. He argued that African Americans needed to unite and fight violence with violence, if nonviolence did not work. Malcolm was now a major political activist. He was no longer the religious fanatic he had been at the height of his involvement in the Nation of Islam.

In early February, 1965, Malcolm traveled to London to address the First Congress of the Council of African Organizations. From there, he left to go to Paris to address the Federation of African Students. However, the French government refused to let Malcolm enter the country because they feared that his speeches might cause the African students in Paris to riot. Forced to return to London, Malcolm spoke at the London School of Economics. Upon returning to New York, he was again faced with the Nation of Islam's lawsuit that would force his family to move from their home. During the years in which Malcolm had worked hard to build the Nation of Islam, he had not accumulated personal wealth. He did not own his own house and he did not have money saved in the bank to take care of his family in case of an emergency.

A Marked Man

As the death threats increased, Malcolm became more concerned with protecting himself and his family. On February 14, around 2:30 A.M., someone drove past their home and threw firebombs through the front window while they slept. Malcolm helped his pregnant wife and four daughters escape without injury, but the house was badly damaged. After he arranged for his family to stay with a neighbor that night, Malcolm had to prepare to fly to Detroit only a few hours after the bombing to

85

The New York City home of Malcolm X and his family after the firebombing on February 14, 1965. (AP/Wide World Photos)

keep a scheduled speaking engagement.

At first, Malcolm was convinced that the Nation of Islam was responsible for the death threats. They he began to wonder if the FBI was trying to stop his activities. After the bombing, his family moved in with some friends, but Malcolm chose to stay in a hotel so that he would not jeopardize the safety of his family and friends. Four days after the bombing, the Nation of Islam won their lawsuit, and Malcolm's family was legally evicted from their house. Malcolm was beginning to feel the tension around him now, more than ever. He sensed that he was not going to live much longer.

The OAAU had organized a rally at the Audubon Ballroom in Harlem on February 21. Malcolm called his wife and told her to come and bring the children. Betty was surprised; earlier, Malcolm had told her not to attend because it was too dangerous. When Malcolm arrived at the Audubon, some people who had arrived early were already seated. In contrast to the regular routine of the Nation of Islam, Malcolm had asked the OAAU members not to search the incoming guests because it might make them feel uncomfortable or frighten them.

Malcolm was normally a very calm person, but on this particular day he was tense and rather uneasy. Because he was under so much stress, he snapped at some of his coworkers. He was also very disappointed that, due to other commitments, none of the guests he had invited were able to attend. Before going onstage to speak, he apologized for his impatience.

Malcolm took the stage amid loud, welcoming applause. Moments after he greeted the audience, however, an argument broke out between two men. While this disturbance distracted the audience's attention, several other men in the front row stood, pulled out guns, and began shooting at Malcolm.

Malcolm's wife and children were also sitting near the front. When the shooting started, Betty immediately threw her children under the bench and laid across them to protect them. She looked up to see her husband falling backward. She tried to go to him, but somebody held her back. When she finally reached him, Malcolm had already died. Betty Shabazz, pregnant, with little or no money and four young daughters depending on her, had seen her beloved husband assassinated.

Louis Farrakhan, Nation of Islam leader, at New York City's Madison Square Garden. (AP/Wide World Photos)

Malcolm X was a martyr at age thirty-nine. More than twenty thousand people came and stood in the rain to view the fallen African-American leader's body in his casket. Actor Ossie Davis gave the eulogy at the funeral. Afterward, the Muslims had their own special Islamic service for their fallen brother.

Three members of the Nation of Islam, Talmadge Hayer, Norman 3X Butler, and Thomas 15X Johnson, were eventually arrested for the murder of Malcolm X. They were all convicted of murder in the first degree and were sentenced to life imprisonment.

Malcolm's assassination is still the subject of controversy. While some argue that the FBI organized the assassination of Malcolm or, at least, was responsible for making matters

Louis Farrakhan and Malcolm X

Minister Louis Farrakhan is the present-day leader of the Nation of Islam. His organization still follows the original separatist teachings of Elijah Muhammad. Farrakhan was first recruited into the Nation of Islam by Malcolm X.

Farrakhan was born Louis Walcott in 1933 in Bronx, N.Y. He was a calypso singer who performed in various nightclubs. After hearing Malcolm X speak at Temple Number Seven in Harlem, he decided to give up the life of a professional musician and become a member of the Nation of Islam. As Louis X, he continued to play his violin for the Nation of Islam, frequently performing its unofficial anthem, "White Man's Heaven Is Black Man's Hell." He was a protégé of Malcolm. He served as an assistant minister to Malcolm at the New York Temple Number Seven. He accompanied Malcolm on his speaking tours and introduced him to audiences. Louis X listened carefully to his mentor's speeches. He studied the way in which Malcolm was able to arouse the emotions of his audiences. Eventually, Malcolm recommended that Louis X be appointed Minister of the Temple in Boston.

In 1964, when Malcolm charged that Elijah Muhammad was an immoral fake who had committed adultery, Louis X unhesitatingly defended Muhammad. He was appointed Minister of Temple Number Seven in New York and replaced Malcolm as Muhammad's spokesman. Louis X constantly attacked Malcolm in the Nation of Islam's newspaper. He wrote: "Only those who wish to be led to hell or to their doom will follow Malcolm. Such a man is worthy of death." Today, Louis Farrakhan admits that he added to the tension and the climate of hate that led to Malcolm's death. He still believes, however, that Malcolm was wrong to criticize Elijah Muhammad, and he says that he would defend Muhammad again if he had to.

worse between Muhammad and Malcolm, most of the evidence supports the theory that the Nation of Islam organized Malcolm's assassination or, perhaps, some angry Muslims acted independently and shot him. Elijah Muhammad and the Nation of Islam, however, strongly denied any involvement. In 1980, Congressman W. Hughes of New Jersey asked the FBI to look further into Malcolm's assassination. However, the FBI reported that there was no new information on Malcolm's death.

Chapter 10

Malcolm's Legacy

The life of Malcolm X was a life of remarkable transformations. The young criminal who indulged in alcohol and drugs became a law-abiding and highly respected leader who practiced and preached self-discipline and self-determination in the African-American community. The dropout whose formal education ended with the eighth grade taught himself to become a formidable speaker who more than held his own in debates at Oxford, Harvard, and other citadels of learning. For young people everywhere, no matter how difficult their circumstances, Malcolm's example should offer hope and encouragement—proof of the possibility of change for the better.

Integrity, Self-Reliance, and Pride

First and foremost, Malcolm was dedicated to improving the social conditions of people of African descent living all over the world. He learned to put others ahead of himself. Despite the fame and adulation he received, he never lost sight of his own imperfections. He constantly examined himself critically to see how he could improve. He publicly acknowledged the mistakes he made and either tried to correct them or learned not to repeat them. Malcolm proved to be a person who always looked for the truth.

Malcolm was very independent and stood up for what he believed. While he was fearless in his analysis of white racism and his criticism of the U.S. government's woeful record on civil rights, he urged African Americans to take control of their own destiny. His philosophy, based on self-reliance,

Malcolm X received an Islamic burial; at right is his widow, Betty Shabazz.
(AP/Wide World Photos)

self-respect, and self-help, is finding a more receptive audience today than it did thirty years ago. Many African Americans— young people, working people, professionals—who still find themselves confronted with racial discrimination, are inspired by Malcolm's example.

Malcolm is also remembered for his unsatisfied thirst for knowledge. Even though he did not finish school, he never abandoned his love of reading. He educated himself by reading books on every subject. He never lost his desire to return to school nor his ambition to become a lawyer. After leaving the Nation of Islam, he commented that if he had the time he would not be ashamed to return to the ninth grade and finish his academic education.

In his speeches, Malcolm commonly used the terms "black" and "Afro-American" when referring to black people in the United States. He played a major role in making these terms popular during an era when they were considered insulting, while terms such as "colored" and "Negro" were more commonly used. Gradually, African Americans adopted these new names and proudly used them to refer to themselves. Slogans such as "black is beautiful" and "black and proud" became common in African-American communities. Malcolm encouraged African Americans to love themselves and appreciate the beauty found in the texture of their natural hair or the shape of their noses and lips. He was intolerant of any form of self-hatred. Malcolm's audiences observed the pride and love he felt for his culture and people and, as a result, they grew to love themselves as well.

A Pan-African Vision

Malcolm was a black nationalist who evolved to become a pan-Africanist—a person who believed that all black people of African descent were Africans no matter where they lived. He argued that, to fight against racism and to bring about the radical changes that were needed for true equality, African Americans needed to have unity among themselves. They could begin to find that unity, he argued, by rediscovering their common African heritage.

Malcolm came to believe that African Americans should regard Africa as their true homeland. At that time, in the early 1960's, most black people in the United States knew little about Africa, and very few identified themselves as Afro-Americans or African Americans. Gradually, however, under the influence of Malcolm and other pan-African thinkers, some African Americans began to wear African clothing. Some changed their names to African ones and gave African names to their newborn children. Others traveled to Africa to find out more about their ancestral culture, while some relocated there to live permanently.

Malcolm came to realize that not all whites were racist or hostile toward African Americans. He realized his error in criticizing white people as being the sole cause of African-American people's problems. He looked more critically at the economic system, capitalism, and argued that this system produced problems such as unemployment and poverty that caused the majority of people to suffer. He began to look more favorably on socialism as an economic system that did not encourage racial discrimination but, instead, unity between people.

The Los Angeles riots in 1992 confirmed Malcolm's prediction that violence and unrest in cities across the United States will continue as long as African Americans and others are victimized by economic as well as racial discrimination. He emphasized the need for African Americans to concentrate on bringing unity among peoples of African descent all over the world in order to gain economic and political power. In his last speeches and interviews, Malcolm explained how the problems of African Americans were no different from many of the problems faced by peoples of African descent all over the world.

Malcolm's pan-African solution to African-American problems went beyond the solutions favored by the moderate leaders of the Civil Rights movement and beyond the borders

A Los Angeles shopping mall owned by Korean Americans burns during the 1992 riots that followed the Rodney King verdict. (AP/Wide World Photos)

of the United States. While most Civil Rights activists did not agree with Malcolm, his pan-African solution was eventually adopted by some of the younger activists. Following the path of other pan-African greats such as W. E. B. Du Bois, Marcus Garvey, and Kwame Nkrumah, Malcolm's ideas were ahead of

Malcolm's legacy is to be found in the lives he touched and the lives he continues to touch long after his death. (AP/WideWorld Photos)

his times. He realized that people of African descent will be free from discrimination and respected throughout the world only when their original homeland, Africa, is free and respected.

Malcolm believed that Africa's strength would remain fragmented as long as it was divided into many countries with different governments under different political and economic systems, lacking both common goals and the power to achieve them. To many Americans, black and white alike, African unity would seem a remote issue, with little bearing on their lives. In Malcolm's global vision, however, the need for African unity was directly related to the everyday issues confronting African Americans. Malcolm's ideas contributed significantly to the larger pan-African movement, while through his work to build the OAAU many others were recruited to pursue unity among African peoples.

A Quiet Storm

Malcolm has become a hero for black people everywhere. Young people particularly admire Malcolm; for them, he is a heroic role model, one who voiced controversial ideas without fear or compromise. They appreciate having an alternative, militant leader to compare to the more moderate or mainstream leaders of both the past and present.

As problems of unemployment, poverty, poor housing, AIDS, and drug abuse continue to haunt African-American communities in the United States, many people, advantaged and disadvantaged, recognize the continuing relevance of Malcolm's message. His words, "by any means necessary," originally used to affirm the right to self-defense against racist violence, have become a motivating slogan for African Americans seeking more assertive means for bringing about positive change in their communities.

When Malcolm X was alive, his words were militant and

angry and alienated many people, both African-American and white; yet his boldness was admired by many, who felt that Malcolm said what they were thinking but were afraid to express. When Malcolm lived, he appeared to be a threatening storm. Decades later, he represents a quiet storm that has slowly unfolded in the lives of many people, influencing their outlook on life and changing their goals and lifestyles. Malcolm still is causing people to reexamine themselves and their society. This is the legacy of Malcolm X.

Speeches and
Writings of Malcolm X

Breitman, George, ed. *By Any Means Necessary*. 2d ed. New York: Pathfinder, 1992. A collection of speeches, interviews, and letters by Malcolm. Among the topics addressed are his split with the Nation of Islam, the OAAU, the role of women, youth, and socialism.

_____, ed. *Malcolm X Speaks: Selected Speeches and Statements*. New York: Grove Weidenfeld, 1990. With one exception, all of the speeches in this substantial collection (first published in 1965) were given by Malcolm in the last year of his life. Among the topics considered are revolution, nonviolence, black nationalism, voting, Africa, and the Civil Rights movement. Includes his classic speech "The Ballot or the Bullet."

Clark, Steve, ed. *February 1965: The Final Speeches*. New York: Pathfinder, 1992. The first volume in a projected series intended to provide a complete and authoritative chronological record of Malcolm's writings, speeches, interviews, and other statements.

Epps, Archie, ed. *Malcolm X: Speeches at Harvard*. New York: Paragon House, 1991. An updated edition of a collection first published in 1968 under the title *The Speeches of Malcolm X at Harvard*. More than half of the book consists of editor Archie Epps's analysis of the evolution of Malcolm's thought.

Gallen, David, ed. *Malcolm A to Z: The Man and His Ideas*. New York: Carroll and Graf, 1992. A heavily illustrated compilation of brief quotations from Malcolm on a wide range of subjects and in a wide range of moods, interspersed with recollections of Malcolm by many people who knew him.

Malcolm X. *Malcolm X on Afro-American History*. New York: Pathfinder, 1991. This speech discusses ancient history, Afro-American history, and American slavery. Includes a question-and-answer segment in which Malcolm talks about the role of black nationalists.

_____. *Malcolm X Talks to Young People*. New York: Pathfinder, 1991. Malcolm talks to young activists about his break with the Nation of Islam; in another speech, he talks with young people in Mississippi about nonviolence and the Civil Rights movement.

Malcolm X with Alex Haley. *The Autobiography of Malcolm X*. New York:

Ballantine, 1992. Written by Alex Haley on the basis of Malcolm's notes and many conversations with him, and first published in 1965 shortly after Malcolm's assassination, this is Malcolm's life story as he told it, from his boyhood in Michigan to his final months.

Perry, Bruce, ed. *Malcolm X: The Last Speeches*. New York: Pathfinder, 1989. Includes several of Malcolm's last speeches and interviews. Provides further insight into how his political views were changing right up to the time of his death.

Time Line

1925   Malcolm Little born on May 19 in Omaha, Nebraska.

1929   Littles buy a house in Lansing, Michigan; father preaches in churches in Michigan and surrounding states and promotes the pan-African philosophy of Marcus Garvey; house burns to ground in September leaving the family unharmed.

1931   Father is run over by a streetcar and dies.

1939   Mother is committed to a state mental hospital; Malcolm is placed in a juvenile home.

1940   Visits half-sister Ella in Boston during the summer; lives in various foster homes in Lansing until 1941.

1941   Moves to Boston to live with Ella; becomes involved in criminal activities.

1943   Moves to New York and works for the railroad occasionally and for Small's Paradise; known as "Detroit Red," he lives a life of drugs and crime.

1944   Returns to Boston; indicted for larceny and given three-month suspended sentence and one year on probation.

1946   Convicted of larceny, breaking and entering, and carrying a weapon and sentenced to eight to ten years in prison; begins serving term in Charlestown Prison and starts a program of intensive reading and self-education.

1947   Converted to the teachings of the Nation of Islam (NOI).

1952   Released from prison; meets Elijah Muhammad in Chicago and receives his "X" from the NOI.

1954   Appointed Minister of the NOI's Temple Number Seven, in New York.

1958   Marries Betty Sanders in January and has first child—a daughter, Attallah—in November.

1959   Travels to the Middle East and to Ghana, Africa, as an ambassador for Elijah Muhammad.

1960   Birth of second daughter, Qubilah, in December.

1962   Learns of Elijah Muhammad's adultery; birth of third daughter, Ilyasah.

1963　Suspended from publicly representing the NOI after commenting on the assassination of President Kennedy.

1964　Meets with Alex Haley to begin collaboration on autobiography; breaks with the NOI and forms a new organization, the Muslim Mosque, Inc.; travels to Mecca and Africa, embracing orthodox Islam and returning to the U.S. with a changed attitude toward whites; announces the formation of the OAAU; returns to Africa for a third time and meets with eleven African heads of state; birth of fourth daughter, Gamilah, in December.

1965　House is firebombed during the night; one week later, on February 21, Malcolm is shot and killed by several assailants during a speech at the Audubon Ballroom in Harlem; three members of the NOI are arrested and later (1966) convicted of the murder; publication of *The Autobiography of Malcolm X*; birth of twin daughters, Malaak and Malikah, in September.

Glossary

Black nationalism: The belief that African Americans should work together for their mutual benefit to create relatively self-sufficient black communities.

Capitalism: An economic system in which the flow of goods and services is determined primarily by supply and demand in a free market and in which capital goods (that is, accumulated goods or wealth) are owned by individuals or corporations. Capitalism is the economic system of the United States.

Civil Rights movement: The organized movement to end discrimination against African Americans, to redress past injustices, and to bring about a society worthy of America's founding vision. Gaining national recognition in the 1950's and 1960's, the Civil Rights movement inspired other groups who were victims of discrimination to claim equal rights under the law.

Hajj: A pilgrimage to Mecca, the holy city of Islam, undertaken by devout Muslims.

Integration: The bringing together of people of different races in every sphere of public life. For example, the Civil Rights movement led to the integration of many schools which, under **segregation**, had been all-white. For Civil Rights leaders such as Martin Luther King, Jr., integration was not merely a legal measure but also a guiding philosophy, aimed at the ultimate goal of a genuinely color-blind society.

Nonviolence: The practice of civil disobedience through nonviolent means, such as marches or sit-ins. Inspired in part by Mahatma Gandhi, leaders of the Civil Rights movement urged demonstrators not to use force, even when they were being attacked by police or racist thugs.

Pan-Africanism: A social, political, and cultural movement based on the belief that all black people of African descent share a common identity and that the fate of black people throughout the world is linked to hopes for African unity.

Segregation: The discriminatory separation of the races, enforced by law or custom.

Socialism: An economic system in which the state owns the means of production and in which private property and free enterprise are strictly limited; ideally, a system intended to eliminate the extremes of wealth and poverty that occur under capitalism.

Stereotype: A widely accepted but false generalization; racial stereotypes, such as the notion that African Americans lack the intrinsic abilities needed to perform certain jobs, are particularly destructive.

Bibliography

Adoff, Arnold. *Malcolm X*. New York: Crowell, 1970. This simplified account of Malcolm's life, written for young readers, tells how he changed from a street hoodlum to a world-famous leader.

Baldwin, James. *One Day, When I Was Lost: A Scenario. Based on Alex Haley's "The Autobiography of Malcolm X."* New York: Dial Press, 1973. Written for a film that was never produced, this screenplay covers Malcolm's life from his teenage years as a hustler and criminal to his leadership role in the Nation of Islam, his conflict with Elijah Muhammad, and his political changes after he left the Nation.

Carson, Clayborne. *Malcolm X: The FBI File*. New York: Carroll and Graf, 1991. Documents the private and public life and activities of Malcolm, beginning in 1953 when he became active in the Nation of Islam. Includes brief historical summaries that are accessible to a young adult audience.

Davies, Lenwood G. *Malcolm X: A Selected Bibliography*. Westport, Conn.: Greenwood Press, 1984. This in-depth bibliography includes books, articles, and audiovisual aids. While most of the materials cited are primarily intended for adult readers, there are a few good selections for youth between the ages of ten and fifteen.

Haskins, James. *Picture Life of Malcolm X*. New York: Franklin Watts, 1975. A simple summary suitable for readers as young as ten. Pages of large-print text alternate with full-page black-and-white photos illustrating the whole span of Malcolm's tragically short life.

Randall, Dudley, and Margaret Burroughs, eds. *For Malcolm: Poems of the Life and Death of Malcolm X*. 2d ed. Detroit: Broadside Press, 1969. These poems, inspired by the life of Malcolm, are suitable for young adult readers. Authors include LeRoi Jones (Amiri Baraka), Sonia Sanchez, Gwendolyn Brooks, Etheridge Knight, and Margaret Walker, among others. Also includes the eulogy given by Ossie Davis at Malcolm's funeral.

Shabazz, Betty. "Loving and Losing Malcolm." *Essence* (February, 1992). Malcolm's widow talks about Malcolm as a husband and a father. Young readers will appreciate Shabazz's personal portrayal of Malcolm, which offers unexpected glimpses of him as both a family man and a lover of children.

White, Florence. *Malcolm X: Black and Proud*. Champaign, Ill.: Garrard,

1975. This book, written primarily for readers from ages eight to eleven, focuses on key incidents in Malcolm's life from his childhood (the burning of the Littles' house in Lansing) to his assassination.

Media Resources

Eyes on the Prize. Video, six 60-minute segments. 1986. *Eyes on the Prize II: America at the Racial Crossroads (1965-1985).* Video, eight 30-minute segments. 1987. Distributed by PBS Video. A powerful overview of the Civil Rights movement and contemporary African-American history; includes an insightful presentation of the life and philosophy of Malcolm and his impact.

Malcolm X. Video, 23 minutes. 1965. Distributed by Carousel Film and Video. Explores the formation and growth of Malcolm's beliefs and values in his transformation from street hustler to inspirational leader.

Malcolm X. Film, 92 minutes. 1972. Distributed by Warner Brothers. This documentary biography features footage of Malcolm's speeches and interviews. Includes coverage of the aftermath of his assassination.

Malcolm X. Film, 199 minutes. 1992. Distributed by Warner Bros. Spike Lee's sweeping film biography of Malcolm, from his boyhood and youth to his assassination. While Lee follows Malcolm's autobiography fairly closely, he makes some changes for dramatic effect; in addition, some important aspects of Malcolm's life, such as the role of his half-sister Ella, are omitted entirely.

Malcolm X: A Collection of Tape-Recorded Speeches. Schomburg Center for Research in Black Culture. These tapes collect speeches which Malcolm made in cities in the United States and abroad at public rallies and forums. Includes "Message to the Grassroots," "The Ballot or the Bullet," "The African Revolution," and "Malcolm X on Afro-American History," among others.

Malcolm X: El Hajj Malik El Shabazz. Video, 60 minutes. 1991. Distributed by National Black Archives of Film and Broadcasting. This film examines the life of Malcolm, beginning with a discussion of his parents' political background. It focuses on Malcolm's political development into an international human activist and pan-Africanist.

Malcolm X Speaks. Film, 55 minutes. 1971. Distributed by Grove Press Film Division. Gil Noble reviews the life and teachings of Malcolm through interviews and documentary footage, describing his growth from the anti-white teachings of the Nation of Islam to understanding that whites were not inherently racist.

Pioneers

MALCOLM X

INDEX

Malcolm X, 16
Marriage and family, 65-70
Mecca, 11, 38, 43, 77-78, 79
Montgomery Bus Boycott, 13
Moorish Science Temple, 43
Muhammad, 38, 43
Muhammad, Akbar, 83
Muhammad, Elijah (Elijah Poole),
    36, 39-48, 65-79, 81, 82-83, 89;
    the Twelve Points of, 40
Muhammad, Wallace, 83
Muhammad Speaks, 65, 82
Muslim Mosque, Inc., 77, 81, 85

Names of Malcolm X, 11, 27, 42, 81
Nation of Islam, 13, 34-37, 38-48,
    65-78, 82-83, 84, 88, 89;
    Malcolm X's break with, 75-78;
    Malcolm X's conversion to,
    34-37
Nkrumah, Osagyefo Kwame, 81, 95
Nonviolence, 14, 68

Organization of African Unity
    (OAU), 82, 84

Organization of Afro-American
    Unity (OAAU), 82, 85, 87, 97

Pan-Africanism, 19, 81, 93-97
Parks, Rosa, 13
Public speaking, skill in, 36-37, 48,
    65-67

Segregation, 12
Self-education, 34-37, 93
Shabazz, Betty (née Sanders; wife),
    66, 75, 87
Slavery, 11, 42
Swerlein, Lois, 23-24

United Nations, 14, 84
Universal Negro Improvement
    Association (UNIA), 18, 19, 43,
    69

Wallace, George, 73
Whites, attitudes toward, 38, 42, 65,
    68, 71, 79, 81-82, 94
Wilkins, Roy, 68
World War II, 32